ACKNOWLEDGEMENTS
Sources of photographs:-
Hamlyn Group Picture Library: front jacket (bottom), front endpapers,
5, 7, 13 (top) 13 (bottom), 14, 16, 17, 18, 20, 24, 38, 40—41, back
endpapers, back jacket; D. J. Murphy (Publishers) Limited: 34; Peter
Roberts: front jacket (top), 26, 27, 43.

The numbers refer to the pages on which the photographs appear.

Published 1973 by
THE HAMLYN PUBLISHING GROUP LIMITED
London · New York · Sydney · Toronto
Hamlyn House, Feltham, Middlesex, England
© Copyright The Hamlyn Publishing Group Limited, 1973
ISBN 0 600 36014 8
Printed in England by C. Tinling & Co. Ltd., Prescot & London.

My Learn to Ride Book

by Robert Owen

Illustrated by Tony Streek
& Peter Kesteven

HAMLYN
LONDON · NEW YORK · SYDNEY · TORONTO

Contents

Introduction

Most boys and girls at some time or another dream of owning their own pony. But for many people, for all sorts of reasons, it is often not possible for that lovely dream to come true. Well, if you are among them, don't despair! After all, being with ponies, learning how to look after and ride them is all that really matters, whether they belong to you or your local riding school.

MY LEARN TO RIDE BOOK will give you the basis for a good all round knowledge and understanding of ponies. Here you will learn how to look after them, groom them and care for their saddlery and equipment, as well as how to actually ride and jump, because these aspects of horsemanship are all equally important and enjoyable. Time spent with a pony, caring for him and simply getting to know him is very satisfying. In return, you will have a lot of fun and the special comradeship that comes from the association with horses and ponies.

Well, now that you are all set to learn to ride, just a few words about the sort of clothes you will need. The only really important item of clothing you must have before starting out on your riding career is a correctly fitting hard hat. It is essential that you wear it wherever and whenever you ride, even if it is only from the field to the stable. Accidents can happen — the pony might stumble and toss you over his shoulder, on to your head. Or, just as easily, you could hit your head on an overhanging branch . . . it simply isn't worth the risk!

Having taken care of that very necessary item, what else will you need? Surprisingly little, for although jodhpurs, riding boots and hacking jackets are all nice to have, you can begin to ride with a strong pair of jeans, leather shoes and a jumper. You can add to your wardrobe as time goes on!

It takes time to build up an understanding between you and your pony. But this, coupled with the good advice you'll find here and your own common sense will introduce you to one of the most natural and satisfying pastimes.

Points of a Horse

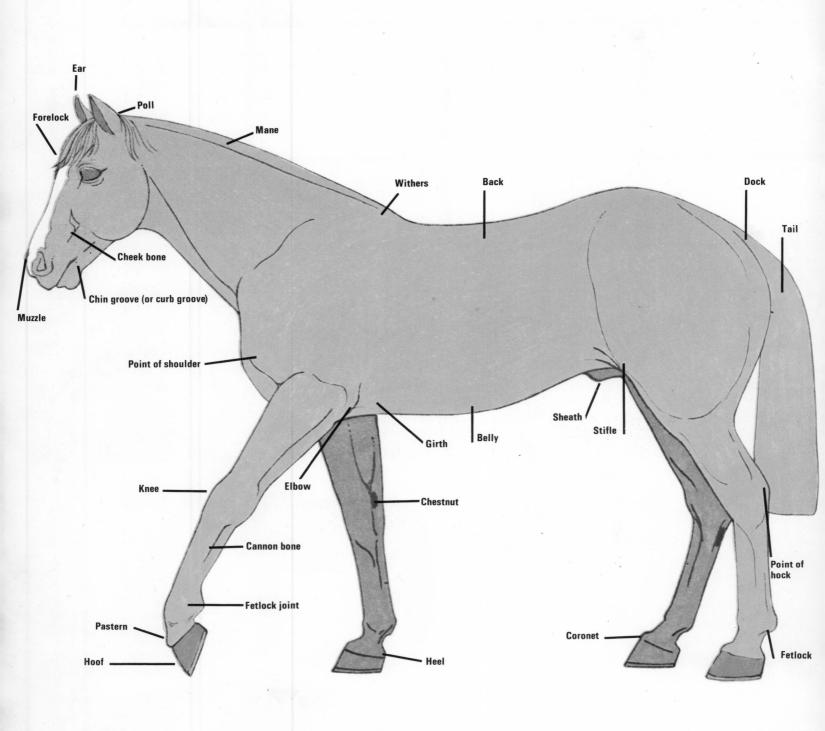

Ear
Poll
Forelock
Mane
Withers
Back
Dock
Tail
Cheek bone
Chin groove (or curb groove)
Muzzle
Point of shoulder
Sheath
Stifle
Girth
Belly
Knee
Elbow
Chestnut
Point of hock
Cannon bone
Fetlock joint
Pastern
Coronet
Fetlock
Hoof
Heel

One of the first things you should learn is the names and positions given to the 'points' of a horse. It is important to be able to recognise these, as they are referred to both in conversation with other riders, and in all instruction books. It will also help to give you an idea of what to look for if you are choosing a pony, although don't imagine that merely by learning the points you will be able to avoid all the pitfalls that are present. However, it will certainly give you a good basis on which to start learning.

The points we have shown here are the most common ones, and ones that every rider should know. As you become more experienced you will also learn to recognise some of the less well-known points.

Age of a Horse

If you don't know your pony's age, you can find out by looking at his teeth. You will have to learn to recognise the shape and marks found in the teeth at varying ages, and the diagrams below will help you do this. To look at his teeth, open the pony's mouth by gently putting your thumb and forefinger on the bar of his lower jaw between the incisor and molar teeth.

Birth – 6 months: the temporary incisors or milk teeth begin to appear after 10 days

2 years: there is now a full set of milk teeth, showing small dark rings on the biting edges

3 years: first permanent teeth. At first they show no marks, but these soon appear

5 years: a 'full mouth' of permanent teeth. Corner incisors meet only at the front

years: corner incisors now meet, and a small hook appears on the upper corner incisors

9 years: 'Galvayne's Groove' appears at top corner incisors. At this age it is about $\frac{1}{8}$ in. long

15 years: teeth have become more triangular and are beginning to slope out

25 years: slope of incisors is very pronounced. Galvayne Groove is disappearing

Measuring

Ponies are measured from the ground to the highest point of the withers. Their height is always given in 'hands' and each hand is 4 inches. If the measurement is more than 14·2 hands high, the animal is called a 'horse' not a pony.

Near- and Off-side

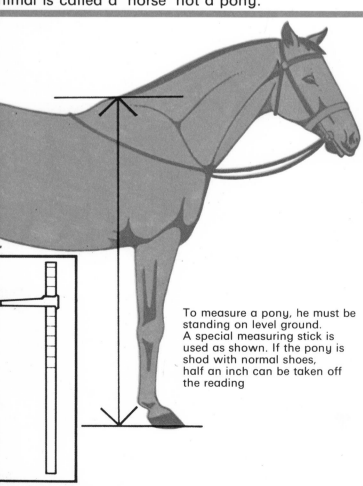

To measure a pony, he must be standing on level ground. A special measuring stick is used as shown. If the pony is shod with normal shoes, half an inch can be taken off the reading

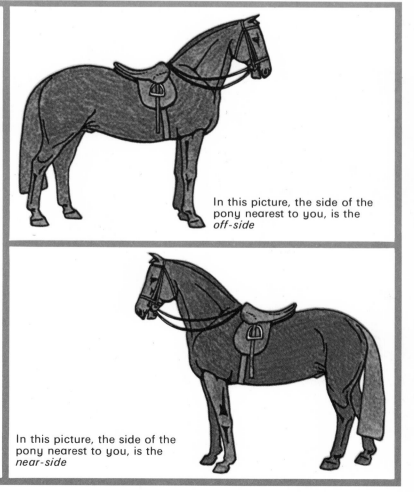

In this picture, the side of the pony nearest to you, is the *off-side*

In this picture, the side of the pony nearest to you, is the *near-side*

What to Avoid

The most obvious points to avoid when choosing a pony are those connected with his conformation — that is, build and appearance. Some common ones are illustrated below. Watch his action carefully when he is moving and avoid a pony with a jerky gait. It may hide a chronic lameness.

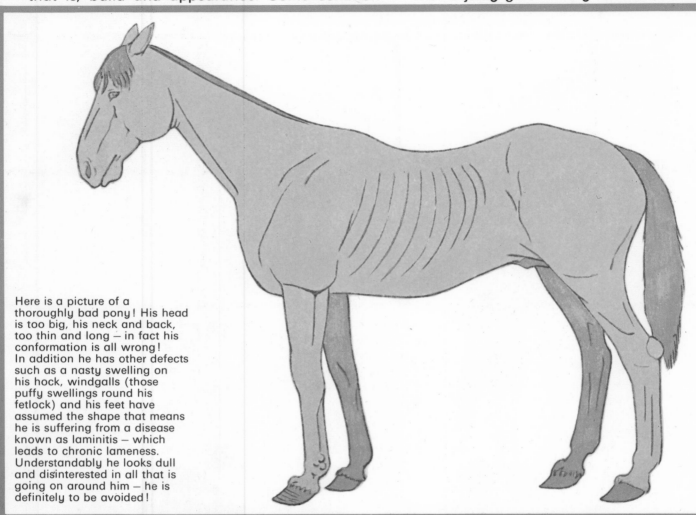

Here is a picture of a thoroughly bad pony! His head is too big, his neck and back, too thin and long — in fact his conformation is all wrong! In addition he has other defects such as a nasty swelling on his hock, windgalls (those puffy swellings round his fetlock) and his feet have assumed the shape that means he is suffering from a disease known as laminitis — which leads to chronic lameness. Understandably he looks dull and disinterested in all that is going on around him — he is definitely to be avoided!

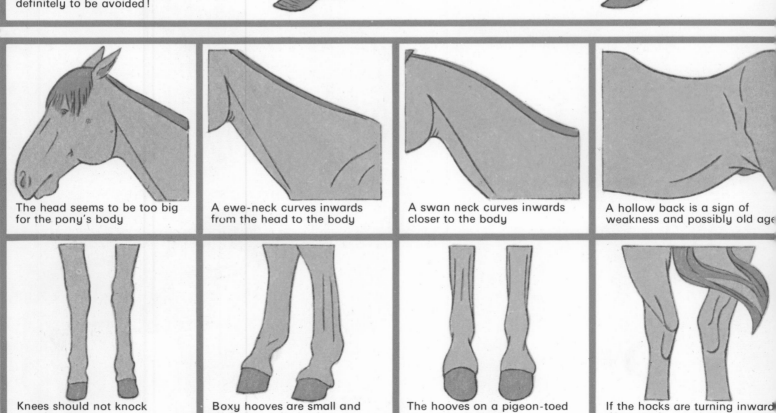

The head seems to be too big for the pony's body

A ewe-neck curves inwards from the head to the body

A swan neck curves inwards closer to the body

A hollow back is a sign of weakness and possibly old age

Knees should not knock together

Boxy hooves are small and similar to a donkey's

The hooves on a pigeon-toed pony turn inwards

If the hocks are turning inward the pony is cow-hocked

What to Look For

If you are buying a pony, the most important thing is to choose a breed that will suit your requirements. In other words, if he is to be kept in a field all the year, and if you just want to hack around with your friends and have fun, don't buy a sensitive, show-type pony!

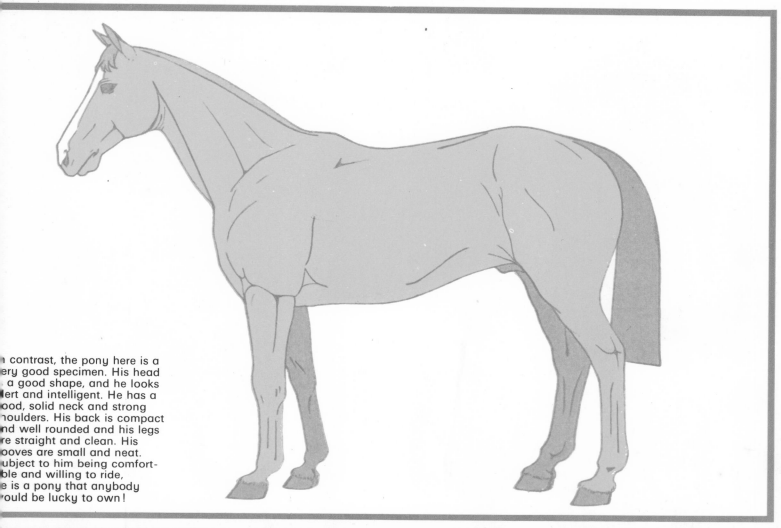

In contrast, the pony here is a very good specimen. His head a good shape, and he looks alert and intelligent. He has a good, solid neck and strong shoulders. His back is compact and well rounded and his legs are straight and clean. His hooves are small and neat. Subject to him being comfortable and willing to ride, he is a pony that anybody would be lucky to own!

A well-proportioned head with kind eyes and pricked ears

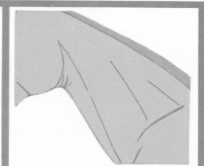

The neck should be solid, but not too short or long

The neck should continue into strong sloping shoulders

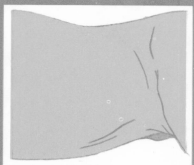

The back should be the right length with a deep girth

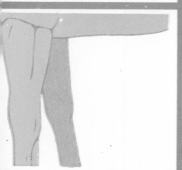

Front legs should be broad at the top, tapering to the knees

Below the knee, the leg should look broad and flat

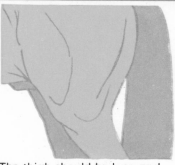

The thigh should be long and muscular

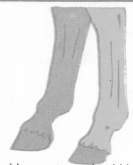

Hind leg pasterns should be less sloping than the front

Colours

Bay

Black

Chestnut

Grey

Palamino

Strawberry Roan

Skewbald

The colour of a pony is not usually in the lea
indicative of how good or bad he is, although son
breeds tend to be specific colours. For exampl
Connemara ponies are usually grey. The mo
common colours for ponies are chestnut, bay ar
grey, all of which can vary in shade. Here is
selection of colours of ponies and horses.

Types of Pony

This is a thoroughbred type of pony, beautiful to look at, but probably not one ideally suited for a beginner to ride. See how well he has been turned out, in fact he looks quite ready for the show ring.

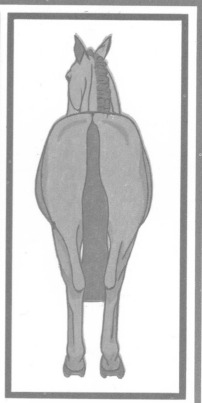

The rear view of a pony is very important. His quarters should be rounded, and his legs, clean and straight.

The Thoroughbred is considered to be the most magnificent type of horse by many people. But it is not suitable for a beginner as it is usually highly strung and easily excited. It also needs more care and attention than most other types of horse.

The Connemara is a sturdy, good looking pony and a native breed from Ireland. It is an excellent pony for children as it has lots of stamina, intelligence and a natural jumping ability. It has become so popular that it is now bred all over the world.

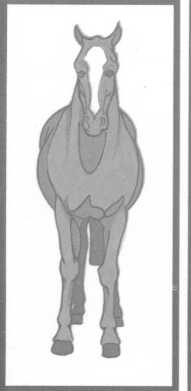

From the front view, the pony's head should be carried high and he should look alert. His chest should be neat, but solid.

The pony pictured here is a good, all-rounder! He is not a thoroughbred, but a thoroughly sensible sort of pony who will have a go at anything and is kind and thoughtful. He is a useful pony for a beginner to learn to ride.

The Cross-Bred pony is a cross between any two different types of pony. If either parent was a thoroughbred, the pony is known as *Part-bred*. Many Cross-bred ponies make excellent riding ponies, but it is a good idea to find out details of the parentage.

Keeping a Pony

If you are going to own a pony you must think carefully about where you are going to keep him. As it is not always easy, particularly in school term-time to give a stable-kept pony all the attention he needs, many children keep their ponies out at grass all the year round. Although this is the easiest way to keep a pony, there are some points to consider. The field should be well drained — not boggy — and should have a good supply of grazing. Fencing should be firm and safe; a wooden post and rails is the best kind, but even this should be checked frequently. There should be constant fresh water and also some shelter in the field (see bottom of page). You should visit your pony every day to make sure he is all right — no stones in his hooves or cuts from low branches, — and also to get him used to seeing you.

If you are going to keep your pony in a stable, make sure it is big enough for him to move round comfortably. It should be light, well ventilated, but free from draughts, and have a good drainage system so that the pony doesn't have to stand on wet bedding. See that he always has enough fresh water and a full hay net to nibble at, otherwise he may start eating his bedding. He will need thorough grooming every day to stimulate his muscles and coat, and at night-time at least, he will need to wear some rugs. It is extremely important to exercise a stable-kept pony every day.

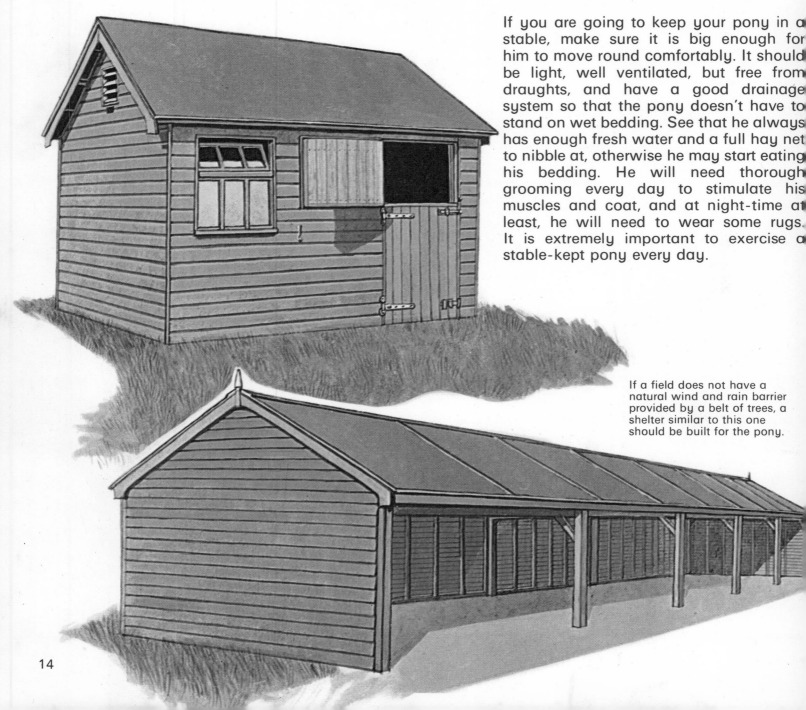

If a field does not have a natural wind and rain barrier provided by a belt of trees, a shelter similar to this one should be built for the pony.

Feeding & Watering

Ponies are not difficult animals to feed providing you remember to follow some simple rules: Always give water before a feed; feed little and often but at regular times; and don't exercise a pony immediately after he has eaten. These things apply whether your pony is kept out at grass or in a stable.

It is difficult to lay down hard and fast rules for feeding; the amount and type of food you give will depend a lot on the size, age and type of pony and the sort of work you expect him to do. If the pony is out at grass, he should not need any extra feed during the summer. During the winter, he should have one or two full hay nets a day and this could be supplemented with a small feed of bran and pony cubes. He should not need oats or corn, and in fact it would not be very good for

him to have these, as they will tend to make him excited and head-strong when he is being ridden.

A stable-kept pony is a different matter altogether, and he will need regular well-balanced feeds of corn and bran. He should also have occasional mashes, and hay should always be provided for him.

A stable-kept pony should have two buckets of fresh water in his box continually. You will probably have to refill these several times a day but it is very important that he is never without clean water.

The best way to provide water for a grass-kept pony is to have piped water operating with a ball-cock into a drinking trough. Make sure the water is always clean and the mechanism is working efficiently.

Stable Management

If your pony is kept in a field with a lean-to shelter, it is a good idea to put some straw on the floor of the shelter. But if your pony is kept in the stable at night, a thick layer of bedding is essential.

The most common form of bedding is straw, wheat straw being the best type. Peat, wood chips and sawdust can also be used.

The first thing to do each morning if the pony has been in the stable overnight is to 'muck-out'. First, tie the pony up on one corner of the stable, or put him out to graze. Using a large garden fork, remove all soiled straw, putting it either into a wheelbarrow, skip (large basket), or on to a large piece of sacking, and take it out to the dung heap. Toss up the rest of the straw and stack it against the

walls of the stable so that it can air during the day. Sweep the floor and allow it to dry.

Some people like to leave a thin covering of straw over the floor if the pony is to be in the stable all day. But at night-time more straw must be spread on the floor so that the bedding is nice and thick. Make sure when you re-make the bed that you pack the straw tightly against the walls. Then hang up a full hay net, fill up the water buckets and put a feed in the manger so that your pony will be comfortable for the night.

If the pony has been put out to graze, it is a good idea occasionally to take all the straw out of the box and swill the floor over with water and disinfectant. Allow the floor to dry.

The picture above shows some smart loose-boxes with a neat, tidy dung heap close by. The dung heap should always be close to the stable, but this means it is even more important to keep it tidy. Make sure that the area around the stable and dung heap is cleaned and swept regularly. Below you can see the straw in a stable neatly stacked against the walls, ready to be spread when the horse is bedded down later on. The floor is being swept clean.

Grooming

The care and attention given to a pony's coat and body is called grooming. Regular, careful grooming not only makes your pony look well cared for, but it also helps to keep him healthy as it stimulates his skin, muscles and blood circulation. Time spent in grooming your pony is essential too, for getting to know and trust one another.

If you keep your pony out at grass, thorough grooming is not so important as if he is stable-kept. In fact in the winter, apart from attention to his hooves, face, mane and tail — the grooming of his body should only be to remove caked and dried-on mud. If you groom his body too much you will brush out the essential oil he needs to protect himself from weather conditions. If he is stable-kept, however, he should be thoroughly groomed every day.

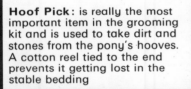

Hoof Pick: is really the most important item in the grooming kit and is used to take dirt and stones from the pony's hooves. A cotton reel tied to the end prevents it getting lost in the stable bedding

Mane Comb: a small metal comb used mainly for trimming the mane. If you actually use it to comb the mane or tail, be very careful. It will quickly tear or break the hair

Curry Comb: is used to clean the body brush after every few strokes across the pony's body. Never should it be used on the pony's body. Clean the comb by tapping it smartly on the stable or yard floor

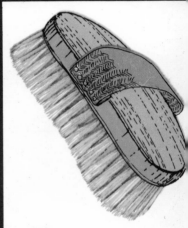

Body Brush: is an oval shaped brush with shorter bristles than the dandy brush. It is used together with the curry comb to groom the pony's body, and also to brush his mane and tail

Dandy Brush: is a brush with long, stiff fibres, used to brush dry mud off the pony's legs. It can be used to remove dried mud or sweat marks from the body, but only on rough coated ponies

Water Brush: is about the same size as a dandy brush, but with softer bristles. It is used to remove stable stains from the body and legs, to wash the hooves, and to dampen the mane and tail to straighten them

Hay Wisp: is made from hay twisted into a rope and wound over to make a double loop. It is used with sharp downward strokes which act as a massage on the pony's skin. It is used before finishing off with the stable rubber

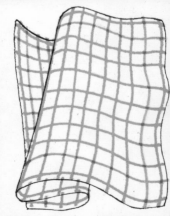

Stable Rubber: is similar to a linen drying-up cloth! It is used to rub firmly over your pony when you have finished grooming him, to give him an extra shine

Eyes and head: Brush the head gently with the body brush, being very careful around the eyes. Squeeze out a sponge with clean water, and sponge the eyes and nostrils carefully. Use a soft sponge, not one that could scratch the pony

Neck: Groom the neck and body with long strokes of the body brush, working from the top of the neck downwards. Using firm strokes, always groom in the direction the hair grows, but don't bang the brush against the pony

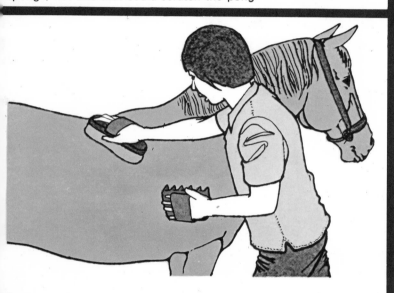

Body: Continue in this way all over the body, always working from the highest point downwards. After five or six strokes, draw the body across the teeth of the curry comb to remove the dust and hair. Brush the legs from the top downwards

Mane: Brush the mane on to the side which it lies naturally, using the body brush. Take a lock of hair in your hand and brush it gently to remove all tangles. Then you can dampen it with the water brush to make sure it lies down. (Do not forget the forelock!)

Tail: Hold the tail in your left hand, and with the body brush, pull a strand of hair away from the rest. Brush this to remove all tangles and then brush down another strand of hair. Continue in this way until you have brushed the entire tail. Sponge the dock

Feet: All four feet must be picked out with the hoof pick. To do this, run your hand down each leg in turn, and lift it by supporting the fetlock joint. Work from the heel to the toe so that you do not hurt the frog. Hooves may be brushed with hoof oil

Clipping

Horses and ponies are clipped in the autumn, but usually only if they are going to be heavily fox-hunted or shown during the winter months.

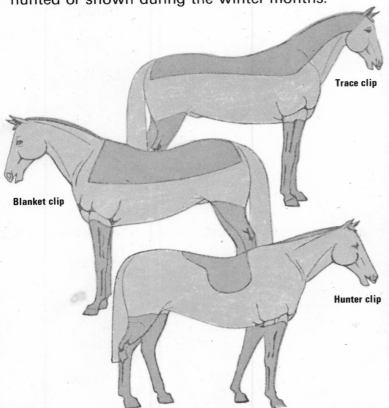

Trace clip

Blanket clip

Hunter clip

Plaiting

Ponies' manes are plaited if they are going to compete in a 'showing' class at a Horse Show, or occasionally when they are being used for fox-hunting. It is not necessary to plait a pony's mane if he is being entered for a jumping competition, although some people like to do this.

If a pony is to be entered for a top-class show, his tail may also be plaited, but this is more complicated and not done as frequently as mane-plaiting.

Divide mane into equal sections (use a mane comb)

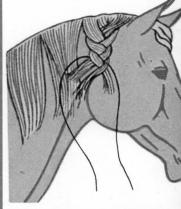

Plait one section at a time — make sure the plait is firm

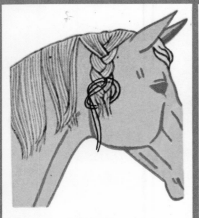

Thread a needle with cotton. Sew round bottom of plait

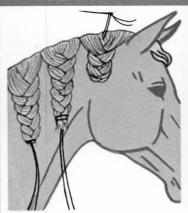

Pass needle through top of plait, so it is folded under

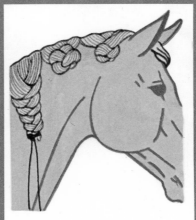

Pass needle down plait and back to top

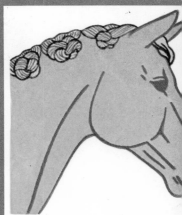

Repeat this process all the way down mane and forelock

Rugs

The best known rugs for ponies to wear are the New Zealand Rug, a waterproof rug worn by ponies out at grass in the winter; a night rug made of jute and a day rug made of woollen material, worn during the night or day by stable-kept ponies; and a summer sheet worn when travelling or at a show to keep a groomed pony clean.

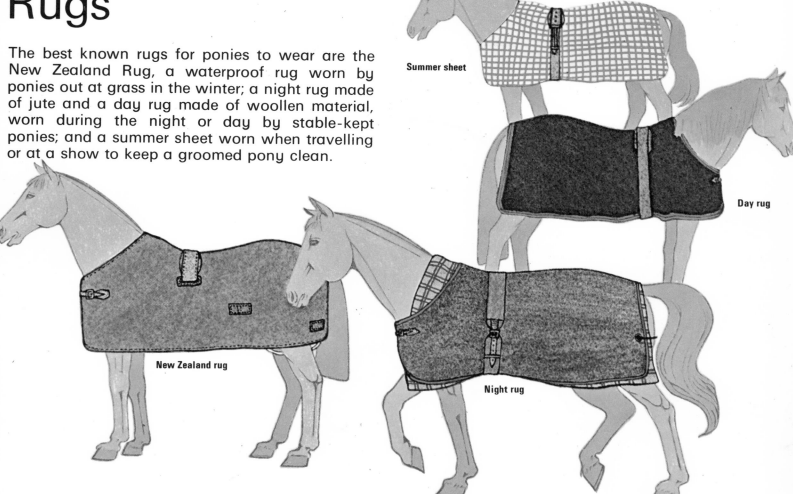

Summer sheet

Day rug

New Zealand rug

Night rug

Bandaging

Ponies' legs are bandaged for two purposes — protection in the stable and during travelling, or to strengthen the legs in exercise. The latter is really only necessary if the pony is expected to gallop and jump on hard ground. Stable bandages are made of flannel, and exercise bandages of crepe which stays on better as it is slightly elastic. The top of the tail can also be bandaged, usually to keep it clean and sleek if the pony is to be shown.

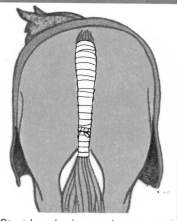

Start bandaging at the top, and wind down to end of dock

Stable bandages are wound over the fetlocks

For exercise bandages, wrap cotton wool round lower leg

Leave length of bandage as shown and fold over top

Bandage to top of fetlock. Turn up extra piece

Bandage up the leg, tying on the *outside*

Bridles

The function of a bridle is to support the 'bit', the metal or rubber bar, in a pony's mouth, which, with the reins, is the main means of controlling a pony. As a pony's mouth is very sensitive, the way that you control the reins is one of the most important factors of good riding. The three most commonly used bridles are the SNAFFLE, the PELHAM and the DOUBLE BRIDLE.

Below left: parts of a double bridle are shown separately. In a bridle which has only one bit, No. 5 — bridoon cheek and sliphead — is not used.

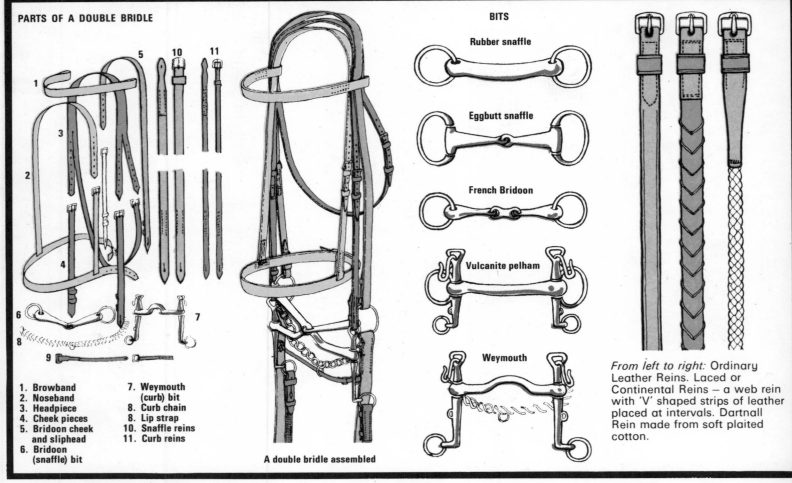

PARTS OF A DOUBLE BRIDLE

1. Browband
2. Noseband
3. Headpiece
4. Cheek pieces
5. Bridoon cheek and sliphead
6. Bridoon (snaffle) bit
7. Weymouth (curb) bit
8. Curb chain
8. Lip strap
9.
10. Snaffle reins
11. Curb reins

A double bridle assembled

BITS

Rubber snaffle

Eggbutt snaffle

French Bridoon

Vulcanite pelham

Weymouth

From left to right: Ordinary Leather Reins. Laced or Continental Reins — a web rein with 'V' shaped strips of leather placed at intervals. Dartnall Rein made from soft plaited cotton.

Stand on pony's near-side, and slip reins over the head

Hold the top of bridle with right hand. Slip bit into the pony's mouth with left hand

Buckle noseband. You should be able to place two or three fingers between the head and the noseband and throatlash

Gently pull the ears through headband. Buckle throatlash

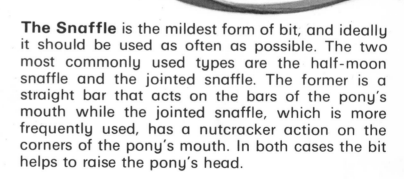

The Snaffle is the mildest form of bit, and ideally it should be used as often as possible. The two most commonly used types are the half-moon snaffle and the jointed snaffle. The former is a straight bar that acts on the bars of the pony's mouth while the jointed snaffle, which is more frequently used, has a nutcracker action on the corners of the pony's mouth. In both cases the bit helps to raise the pony's head.

The Double Bridle is a combination of a snaffle-type bit and a curb bit. A curb bit has a 'curb chain' that is secured behind the pony's chin, and makes him bend his head inwards from the poll. The snaffle again raises the pony's head to the right position. These two actions make it an ideal bridle to use when showing a pony.

The Pelham combines the action of the snaffle and curb in just one bit. It has two reins attached to it — the top makes the bit perform the same action as the snaffle, while the bottom rein operates the curb chain.

Saddles

The saddle is the piece of equipment placed on the pony's back to make it easier and more comfortable for you to ride. There are different types of saddle, but the one you will come across most frequently is the all-purpose saddle.

As you will know the outside appearance of a saddle is smooth leather, but the main inner frame, found in all saddles, is the 'tree'. It is made up of wood and metal and its purpose is to make sure that nothing touches the pony's spine. It is padded and stuffed with webbing, serge and horsehair before being covered with leather.

It is very important that a saddle fits a pony exactly. Badly fitting saddles will not only make ponies uncomfortable and probably disagreeable, but can cause actual injury. The white marks you sometimes see on a pony's back close to the withers, indicate old saddle sores. If your pony develops a saddle sore, you simply cannot ride him until the hair has grown over again, and it always grows in tell-tale white.

The most important thing in fitting a saddle is to make sure no part of it touches the spine.

The pommel (see diagram on next page) should be just behind the rise of the withers and should not pinch them. If the underneath of the saddle is resting on the loins, it is too far back.

To 'saddle-up' a pony, stand on the near side and put the saddle high up on the withers letting it slide back into place. This way the hairs on the back will not be rubbed up the wrong way. Go round to the other side to make sure the flap and girth are not tucked under the saddle. Return to the near side, pull the girth under the pony's tummy and do it up gradually, making sure you do not pinch his skin. Never pull the girths up too tightly at this stage, you should always check them again when you have mounted.

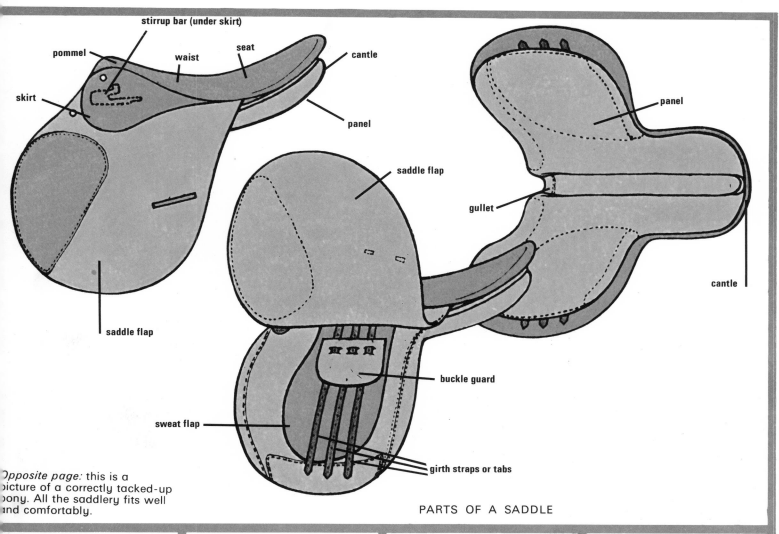

stirrup bar (under skirt)

pommel

waist

seat

cantle

skirt

panel

saddle flap

saddle flap

panel

gullet

cantle

buckle guard

sweat flap

girth straps or tabs

Opposite page: this is a picture of a correctly tacked-up pony. All the saddlery fits well and comfortably.

PARTS OF A SADDLE

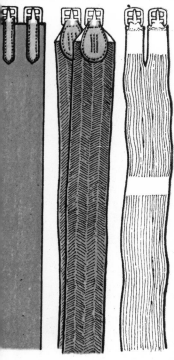

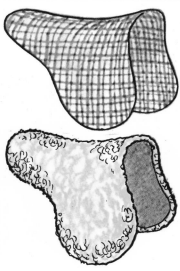

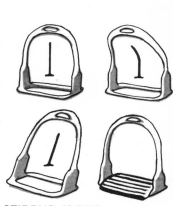

STIRRUP IRONS
From left to right (top): Plain Hunting Iron — the most commonly used type of iron. The Bent Top Iron — the top bends away from the instep making it easier to keep the heel pressed down.
(bottom): The Australian Simplex Pattern Safety Iron — has a forward bulge which is placed on the outside of the foot and allows the foot to be released quickly if necessary. Plain Iron fitted with Rubber Tread — this prevents the foot slipping out of the iron.
The type of iron used is really a matter of personal preference. Stirrup irons, whatever the type, should be made of stainless steel.

GIRTHS
Left to right: a Leather Girth, which is the most expensive, but best sort to use. Webbing Girths, always used in pairs. They must be washed regularly as they become hard with sweat. A Nylon Cord Girth, which is inexpensive and satisfactory.

NUMNAHS
Numnahs are used underneath the saddle, to give added comfort to the pony's back. They should not be used, however, as a permanent protection against a badly fitting saddle. If this is the case, something should be done about the saddle! The most common numnah is the sheepskin one, pictured at the bottom, but it is difficult to keep clean. The numnah at top of page is made from heavy linen. It is used to keep the underside of the saddle clean.

STIRRUP LEATHERS
Stirrup leathers are the strips of leather used on either side of the saddle to hold the stirrup irons. As they tend to stretch with use, they need constant careful checking to make sure they are not getting worn. The picture at the top shows a saddle with irons 'run up' the stirrup leathers.

Care of Tack

The cleaning and care of your pony's saddlery or 'tack' is an important part of horsemanship. Badly cared for and dirty saddlery not only looks unattractive, but it can also be extremely dangerous. If leather is not kept supple by regular cleaning, it soon becomes dry and could break under any pressure. If the bit is not washed off after each ride, the dirt that accumulates will harden and rub against the pony's mouth making it sore. Similarly if sweat is allowed to dry on the underneath of the saddle and girth, it also becomes hard and will rub against the pony's back and tummy. Before you know where you are, you will be dealing with back and girth sores instead of going for pleasant rides.

Regular cleaning of tack acts as a safety measure in another way. As you examine it you will soon notice if stitching is coming undone, buckles are coming loose or there are any gaps under the saddle where the stuffing is beginning to creep through. By having these things put right you could prevent a nasty accident. The state of your tack is an indication too, of just how much care and attention you give your pony.

Large stables, like those at riding schools, have tack rooms, where all the saddles and bridles, spare stirrups, bits and so on, are kept. A bright, tidy tack room where all the saddlery is clean and shiny is a delight to see. Look how pleasant the one in the picture looks — it contains harness belonging to some huge draught horses that are nowadays mostly only seen at horse shows. A tack room is a good place to keep your pony's rosettes, too, which look attractive pinned up on the wall.

Pictured above is all the basic equipment you need to clean your tack. Wash the sponges out thoroughly after you have used them, and keep all the equipment together in a bucket or bin.

Having stressed the importance of keeping your tack in good condition, the thing to do now is to get down to cleaning it. As you can see from the picture above, it can be fun!

The equipment you need is pictured on the left — a bucket, two sponges, a brush, dry cloths, saddle soap and a tin of metal polish. First of all take the stirrup leathers and girth off the saddle, and the stirrup irons from the leathers. Stand the saddle on its pommel (never lay it flat on the ground as this will eventually make the tree spread) and if there are some handy hooks on the wall, hang up the leathers and girth.

Undo all the buckles on the bridle (but make sure you know how to put them all together again) and then hang up all the pieces, or lay them out on a clean patch of ground or a table.

Wash the bit and stirrups, dry them and leave them on one side. If the underneath of the saddle is made of material, brush it to remove dirt and hairs. Then wash all the leather — saddle and bridle. To do this, dip a sponge into the water, and then squeeze it out well. Rub all the separate bits of leather well, frequently re-wetting and squeezing out the sponge. Remember, don't get the leather too wet.

Moisten the other sponge, coat it with saddle soap and rub the soap into all the leather of the saddle and bridle. There should be a very small amount of lather while you are doing this, and the important thing is to rub the soap well into the leather. In fact, elbow grease is more important than using lots of saddle soap!

When you have soaped all the leather, rub it over with a soft, dry cloth to bring up the shine. Polish the stirrup irons with metal polish, and then re-assemble all the pieces together and put your tack away.

Here are a few dos and don'ts for tack cleaning: Do clean your tack each time you have used it, particularly if it has got wet. If you don't have time to do it really thoroughly, wash off the bit, and make sure the girth and underneath of the saddle are clean.

Don't clean the bit, particularly the mouthpiece, with metal polish.

Don't use very hot water, *or* soak leather in water *or* wash it in soda or harsh soap.

Don't make leather too wet.

Mounting

The pictures on this page show how to mount your pony from the near-side, which is the most usual side to mount. When you get more experienced, you should practise mounting from the off-side also. It is important that your pony should stand still while you are getting on him and you can teach him to do this by not actually mounting if he tries to walk away. Talk to him quietly keeping a firm hold on the reins, but on no account jab him in the mouth by pulling on the reins. As always the aids to use to make your pony obey you, are patience and understanding.

Check that the girths are tight. Stand with your left shoulder next to the pony's neck and hold the reins firmly in your left hand, just in front of the withers. Put your left foot into the stirrup iron, which you can hold with your right hand

Still holding the reins firmly, take hold of the pommel of the saddle with your right hand and swing your body round so that you are facing the side of the pony. Press your left toe downwards so that it does not dig into the pony's side

Spring up off the ground, move your right hand to the right hand front of the saddle, and swing your right leg over the pony's back being careful not to kick him

Lower yourself slowly into the saddle, so that you do not come down with a bang. Put your right foot into the stirrup and adjust the length of your stirrup leathers, if necessary

Dismounting

The pictures on this page show you how to dismount, again on the near-side. It is important that your pony stands still for this manoeuvre. If you try to dismount while he is moving, you could find yourself being thrown off balance, and landing on the ground, with your pony galloping off.

When you have dismounted, loosen the girth and run the stirrup irons up the underneath part of the leather so that they rest against the buckle at the top, next to the saddle. This way they will not bang against your pony's side and he will be far more comfortable.

Making sure the pony is standing still and quiet, take both feet out of the stirrups

Hold the reins firmly in your left hand at the withers. Put your right hand towards the back of the saddle on the right hand side

Turn the body slightly towards the pony's off-side. Taking the weight of your body on both hands, swing your right leg over the pony's back. Make sure you don't kick him with your right foot at this stage!

You should then be able to vault lightly off the pony and land on your toes! Run the stirrup irons up the inside of the leathers, so that they rest against the saddle. Take the reins over the pony's head and quietly lead him to the stable or field

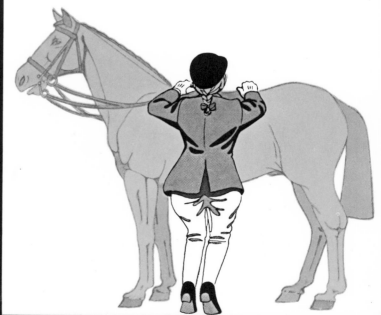

Aids

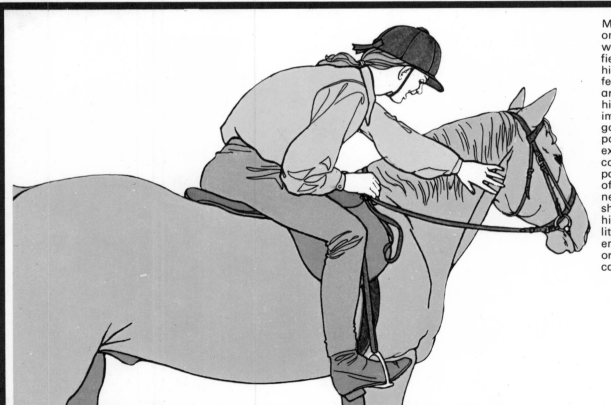

Many people think that the only times to talk to a pony are when they go to him in the field or when they are with him in the stable, grooming or feeding him. As soon as they are actually riding, talking to him immediately becomes less important. However it is a very good habit to talk to your pony while you are riding and exercising him. Talking, combined with a sympathetic pat on the pony's neck, is one of the best ways to soothe a nervous animal, and will also show him you are pleased with him You can use the pat a little more strongly to encourage him to work harder, or to prevent him from carrying out a false move

'AIDS' are the signals given to a pony to tell him what he should do. He should have been trained to understand these while young, and if the signals are given correctly and sympathetically, he will respond to them.

Aids fall into two groups — natural aids and artificial aids. Natural aids are those given with the hands, legs, body and voice. Artificial aids include the use of whips, spurs and more complicated pieces of saddlery, such as martingales. All of these should only be used by experienced riders who understand their use completely.

Aids are given in conjunction with one another. You never just give an aid with your hands for example, it is always given at the same time as a corresponding aid with your legs, and ideally your body and voice as well. This is the best way to get your pony to do what you want smoothly and to ensure that you get him moving 'on the bit'. This means that he is supple, his hindlegs and forelegs are moving in co-ordination and he is ready to respond to whatever you tell him to do. All your aids should be as light as possible, and not visible to an onlooker.

The Hands guide the pony and, to a large extent, control his pace. But sympathetic hands should always be used in conjunction with aids given by the legs. As the slightest movement of the hands reflects on the pony's mouth, they must be used very carefully. The rider in our picture is carrying a whip, held correctly

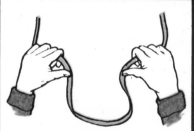

When you are seated, take a rein in each hand, either side of the pony's neck and just in front of the saddle. Place hands on top of the reins

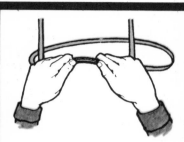

Bring hands together, placing the left rein on top. Let the loop of the reins hang down on the pony's off-side

A side view of hands holding reins correctly. If it is more comfortable you can put your little finger between the rein and loop

Holding double reins correctly. Hands should be kept low, just at the point of the wither, with the backs parallel to the slope of the pony's shoulders

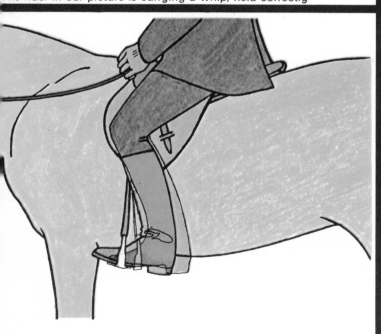

The Legs are used to create energy and impulsion in the pony, and they help to guide the hind-quarters. Leg aids should be given firmly (this doesn't mean kicking your pony sharply in the ribs!) and usually just before you give a corresponding aid with your hands. Make sure your heels are not in contact with your pony's side unless you are giving him an aid

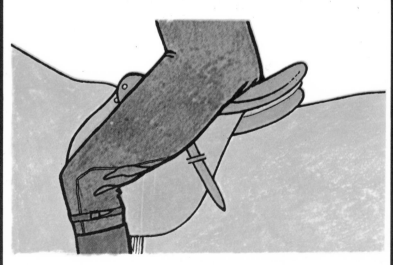

The Body often gets overlooked as a direct aid, but it is, in fact, very important. Your pony will be very sensitive to movement in your body, and the way you distribute your weight will be interpreted by him as an instruction. The weight of your body should be very slightly leaning in the direction of the movement, but be careful not to overdo this, or you could throw him off balance. A good rule to remember is to keep your shoulders square with your pony's shoulders. The contact and pressure of your seat on the saddle is also important in certain aids

31

Learning to Ride

A pony has four natural gaits or paces; the walk, trot, canter and gallop. The walk is a pace of four separate beats; the trot — two beats; the canter — three beats and the gallop — four beats. The gallop is the fastest pace of all and should not really be used unless the rider has a lot of experience and practice and there is sufficient wide open space available!

Besides performing these paces naturally, a well-trained pony can also be made to perform 'collected' or 'extended' paces. However, the rider needs to be quite experienced before attempting to give the right aids, and it is important to master the correct riding position and aids for ordinary paces before trying anything more advanced!

When you have given your pony an aid to increase or decrease his pace, you must make him obey. Don't change your mind because he wants to do something else.

Walk

Having mounted, test the girths to see they are tight, and the leathers to see they are the right length. To do this keep your pony still while you make sure you are sitting correctly. Sit well down into the centre of the saddle, your back straight, your head up (look between your pony's ears), your knees and thighs pressed against the saddle and the lower part of your leg free. Keep your heels lower than your toes, and in a straight line down from your elbow. Hold the reins as described on page 31. When you are ready to move,

Trot

To move from a walk into a trot, keep the riding position you have been practising, and apply more pressure with the lower part of your legs. If your pony is very eager, you can gather the reins in a fraction. There are two ways to ride at a trot — 'rising' or 'sitting'.

The sitting trot is always used when making the transition from one pace to another as it enables the rider to keep in closer contact with the pony. The rising trot, as its name implies, is when the rider rises up and down from the saddle in time with the pony's hoofbeats.

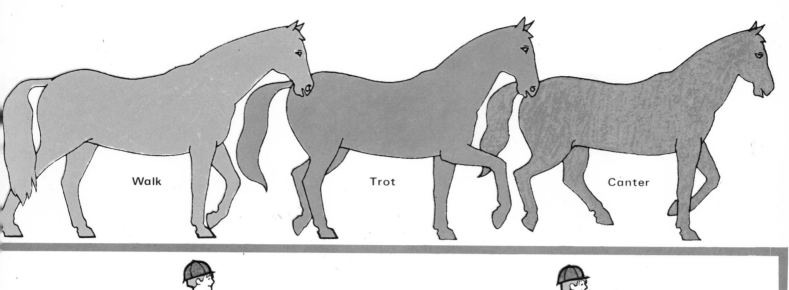

Walk   Trot   Canter

squeeze the pony's sides with your lower legs and gently collect up the reins. Allow the pony freedom of his head, and relax even though you are sitting up straight and alert. To bring your pony back to a halt, sit well into the saddle, close your lower legs and

gently rein-in. The action of your legs and body will push the pony up so that he feels the resistance of your hands. As soon as he responds, ease the reins and relax your body. Remember never to pull on the reins without giving him aids with your legs also.

This is the usual way to ride at the trot, and the most comfortable for both parties! Your body position stays the same, that is your back is kept straight (don't lean forward) and your lower leg should keep still. Don't rely on the stirrups to help you rise up and down, the

grip of your knees and thighs should support you! To slow up, use the same aids as described above, exerting slightly more pressure on the reins if necessary. If you want to bring him to a halt, allow him to walk a few paces first and re-apply the aids.

Learning to Ride cont.

Canter

As the canter is a three-beat pace, the pony can lead with the near-fore or off-foreleg. If he is cantering in a circle, he should lead with the inside leg (see next page), but if he is cantering in a straight line, as long as he is cantering 'true' it does not matter which leg leads.

A pony is cantering true when the leading foreleg and leading hind leg appear to be on the same side. If they appear to be on opposite sides, he is cantering 'disunited'. To move from a trot into a canter, make sure your pony is well collected and responding to any

These people are out for a morning gallop across the downs. They are all in full control of their horses, leaning slightly forward with their reins held a little further forward than usual.

pressure on the reins. Sit down into the saddle so that you are doing a sitting trot. Increase the pressure of your lower legs just behind the girth. Sit well down when cantering, so that you keep close contact with the saddle. Don't lean forward, or you will find you have no control, particularly if your pony starts to go faster. You use the same aids as before to bring him back to a trot, walk or halt. Always apply them gently and gradually, easing the reïns slightly as he comes down to a trot, and again when he comes back to a walk.

A pony is said to be cantering 'on the right' or 'on the left', depending upon which leg is leading. If you watch a pony cantering you will be able to notice quite easily which leg is leading. When you are cantering in a circle, during exercise periods, your pony should lead with the leg on the inside of the circle.

The illustrations above show ponies cantering and leading with the left leg (illustration on right) and the right leg (illustration on left). If you want to make your pony canter with the left leg leading, these are the aids you must give him. First make sure he is trotting in a collected way, ready to respond to whatever aid you give him. Turn his head *very* slightly to the left, sit well into the saddle and keeping your shoulders square with his, *very* slightly lean your body to the left also. Close your left leg on the girth, and take your right leg a little further back also applying pressure. And your pony should lead smoothly off into a canter! If you want him to canter leading with the right leg, simply reverse these aids, so that his head is inclined slightly to the right, your right leg applies pressure on the girth, and your left leg slightly behind it. Practise leading off on to either legs, making sure that the transition is always smooth.

You should also practise making your pony canter off leading with one leg for a few paces, bringing him back to a trot and then making him lead off with the other leg. As you become more experienced, you can bring him back from a trot to a collected walk and make him strike off into a canter from that pace. This is quite an advanced exercise, so make sure you really know what you are doing before you tackle it. It is best to really master the riding position, and the aids for cantering from a trot before attempting anything else.

Exercising

Every time you ride your pony, you are 'exercising' him. The kind of exercise he gets will depend on where you take him and what work you make him do. On the left are the four main types of exercise a pony has — being ridden on the roads, bridle paths, across fields and in a specially marked out school. To a certain extent, a pony also exercises himself when he is kept out at grass, particularly if he is with other ponies.

Whenever you take your pony out for a ride, try to spend some time doing definite exercises, changing legs while cantering, coming back to a halt and so on. Even when you are just hacking on bridle paths it is a good idea to do this, and it is important that your pony does what you want him to do, not what he wants to do. Practise such things as riding away from your friends and going straight past the entrance to his field.

Some trotting on roads is good for your pony, but don't overdo this as it could soon jar his legs. Similarly, never ride too fast on hard ground — even in a wood or bridle path.

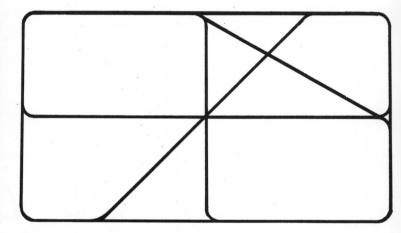

Now and again try to exercise your pony in a 'school' or an even patch of field, preferably with an expert instructing you. You should practise turning corners and riding diagonally across the school — at all paces.

This is a good time also to practise riding in circles, again at a walk, trot and canter. For circles and turns, put slight pressure on the rein in the direction you want to go, sit well into the saddle, and close your legs against the pony's side.

Lungeing and Long-reining

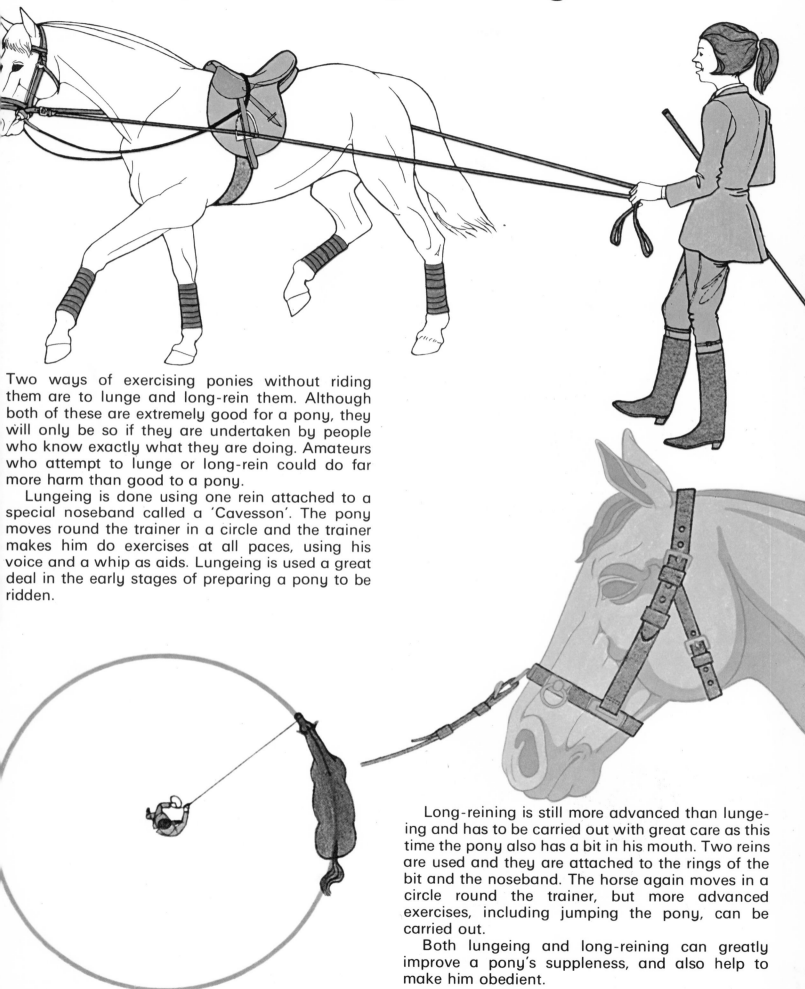

Two ways of exercising ponies without riding them are to lunge and long-rein them. Although both of these are extremely good for a pony, they will only be so if they are undertaken by people who know exactly what they are doing. Amateurs who attempt to lunge or long-rein could do far more harm than good to a pony.

Lungeing is done using one rein attached to a special noseband called a 'Cavesson'. The pony moves round the trainer in a circle and the trainer makes him do exercises at all paces, using his voice and a whip as aids. Lungeing is used a great deal in the early stages of preparing a pony to be ridden.

Long-reining is still more advanced than lungeing and has to be carried out with great care as this time the pony also has a bit in his mouth. Two reins are used and they are attached to the rings of the bit and the noseband. The horse again moves in a circle round the trainer, but more advanced exercises, including jumping the pony, can be carried out.

Both lungeing and long-reining can greatly improve a pony's suppleness, and also help to make him obedient.

Starting to Jump

Ponies are natural jumpers. If they are free they will pop over low jumps in their path rather than go round them and providing they are treated properly, they will continue to enjoy jumping even when they carry a rider on their backs.

The picture below shows a pony's action when he is jumping free. As he comes towards the jump he will lower his head and stretch his neck. This allows him to balance himself in preparation for making the jump. As he takes off he raises his neck and head, and brings his hind legs under his body. He lifts his forelegs off the ground springing upwards and forward. His hind legs then also leave the ground and the pony becomes suspended over the jump, his body forming an arc. His head and neck are stretched as far forward as possible, and hind and forelegs are tucked under his body. As he lands, he brings his head up and stretches out his fore legs to keep his balance. His hind legs land immediately behind the forelegs and he is ready to move off again.

The most important thing to remember when you jump a pony is to let him maintain this natural action as much as possible. For example, you must let him have his head as he goes over the jump so that he can stretch his head and neck to the full extent. Any interference with his natural movement could easily make him stumble over the jump. However, there are some exercises to do before you jump your pony, even over low jumps.

The first step in learning to jump, elementary though it sounds, is to get your pony walking and trotting freely over poles laid on the ground. You will find that even going over poles at this level, a pony will automatically stretch and lower his head. Keep the riding position that you have been taught for these paces, but make sure you follow the pony's head movement with your hands, allowing him the freedom he wants.

The poles should be about 5 feet apart on the ground, although this could vary slightly according to your pony's stride. Practise walking over a line of 6 or 8 of them. Then try trotting over them, at a rising trot. Make sure that you keep close contact with the pony at all times, so that he keeps going in a straight line at a regular pace.

When you feel happy about this, you can go on to the next step — jumping over 'cavelletti'.

The Use of Cavelletti

'Cavelletti' are long straight poles attached at either end to two pieces of wood joined in an 'X' shape. The height of the cavelletti can be varied according to how the 'X' is placed on the ground.

They are very useful pieces of equipment and having got your pony to walk and trot over poles on the ground, the next step is to get him trotting freely over a line of 4 or 6 cavelletti. Again, depending upon the length of the pony's stride, the cavelletti should be about 5 feet apart.

Trotting over cavelletti is a very good exercise for both pony and rider and even international riders school their horses over cavelletti regularly. However, it will help you if there is an expert to watch and instruct you, and in fact someone should be present at all your jumping lessons and practice.

In the pictures below, you can see the many uses of cavelletti, and the different exercises you can perform with them. By placing them on top of one another, you can make larger jumps and spreads as you progress.

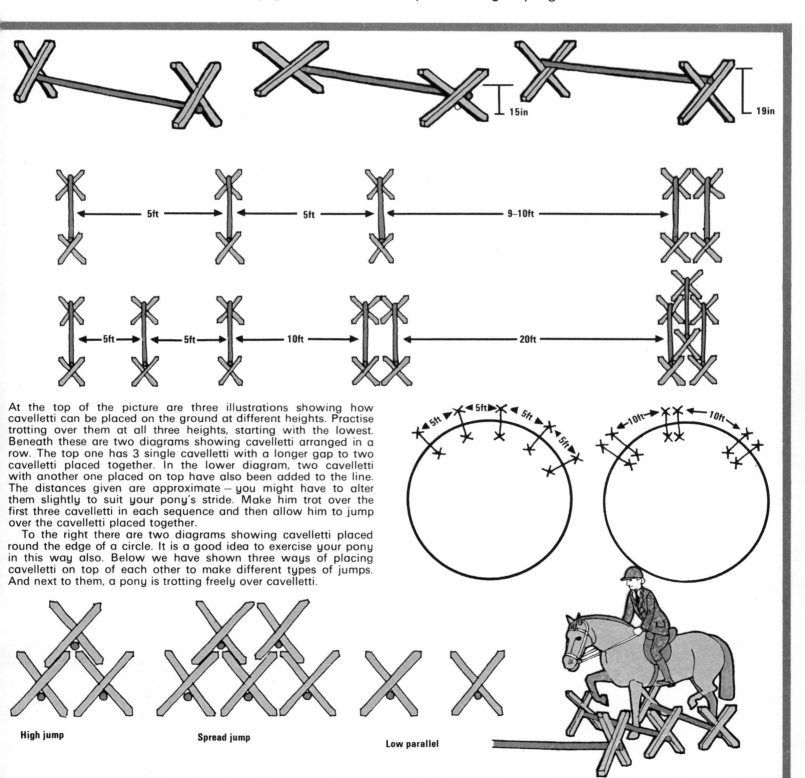

At the top of the picture are three illustrations showing how cavelletti can be placed on the ground at different heights. Practise trotting over them at all three heights, starting with the lowest. Beneath these are two diagrams showing cavelletti arranged in a row. The top one has 3 single cavelletti with a longer gap to two cavelletti placed together. In the lower diagram, two cavelletti with another one placed on top have also been added to the line. The distances given are approximate — you might have to alter them slightly to suit your pony's stride. Make him trot over the first three cavelletti in each sequence and then allow him to jump over the cavelletti placed together.

To the right there are two diagrams showing cavelletti placed round the edge of a circle. It is a good idea to exercise your pony in this way also. Below we have shown three ways of placing cavelletti on top of each other to make different types of jumps. And next to them, a pony is trotting freely over cavelletti.

High jump

Spread jump

Low parallel

Practice Jumps

Now you can start jumping low fences, but remember that you should never leave exercises over poles on the ground and cavelletti behind. Always do them when you exercise your pony in the field.

The aids and positions for jumping during approach, take-off, landing and collection after the jump are explained on the next two pages. Study these thoroughly for they apply however high or wide the jump may be.

Get some friends to help you build practice jumps in the field. Some examples are shown at the bottom of the page. You can use straw bales piled on top of one another, hedge cuttings stacked on the ground, cut-down trees, old car tyres hung from a pole and suspended between supports, oil drums laid on their sides or a variety of other things. Use your imagination but remember to follow a few simple rules.

Practise jumps, particularly in the early stages should not be more than 2 feet to 2 feet 6 inches high. The top of the jump should be smooth with no jagged points or nails sticking up to scratch the pony's leg. It is best if you can erect 'wings' with the jump as this will help to prevent the pony from running to one side as he approaches the jump.

To help pony and rider to judge the take-off position, place a pole on the ground in front of the jump. As you get more experienced you can take this away.

It is good experience also to place a number of jumps in a lane like the one illustrated on the next page. Put up different types of jumps with different spacing between them and as you get better, practise jumping without stirrups — (that will see how good your balance is!). However, don't always jump in a straight line as this tends to excite ponies. Arrange other jumps in the field in a 'course' and practise jumping over them in different sequences, turning corners and riding in circles. This way your pony will not automatically know the way to go each time.

As you begin to feel more ambitious, don't just make the jumps higher. It is better for both of you to increase the spread of the jump. Place another pole the same height on the landing side, or move the ground line further away from the jump. It will help to make the pony spread himself out.

Cardinal rule to remember is 'all things in moderation'. Jumping is fun, but never go on until your pony is bored and just following a routine. It should be fun for him too!

A pony jumping happily over a practice jump of painted oil drums. Pictured on either side are different types of jumps.

Jumping Technique

As you approach a jump, make sure you are sitting well down in the saddle with your knees and thighs gripping firmly. Two or three full strides before you want your pony to take off, close your lower legs against his side, and then give him a sharper squeeze when you want him to actually leave the ground.

As your pony raises his forelegs off the ground, try and keep contact with the saddle with your seat, but move forward with him from your waist, (again the grip comes from your knees and thighs, don't use the stirrups to balance you). Move your hands up and slightly to either side of the pony's neck so as to give him freedom of his head. You should still be looking straight ahead between his ears, not down at the jump.

Keep the same position during suspension, possibly allowing him even more freedom of his head if he wants it. (Your arms and the reins should be in a straight line.) Make sure that your legs are now in the correct position, not sticking forward or back. As the pony's hind legs touch the ground, he will bring up his head to balance himself. Gradually bring back your hands also so that you have control of him. You will find that your weight will also come back to the saddle and you should return to the normal riding position. One of the most important things in jumping is to maintain contact with the saddle with your seat all the time.

A young rider clears a jump in the show ring with ease. She i allowing the pony complete freedom of his head and as a resul he is jumping well and happily. Her own position is quite good although her knees should be closer to the saddle.

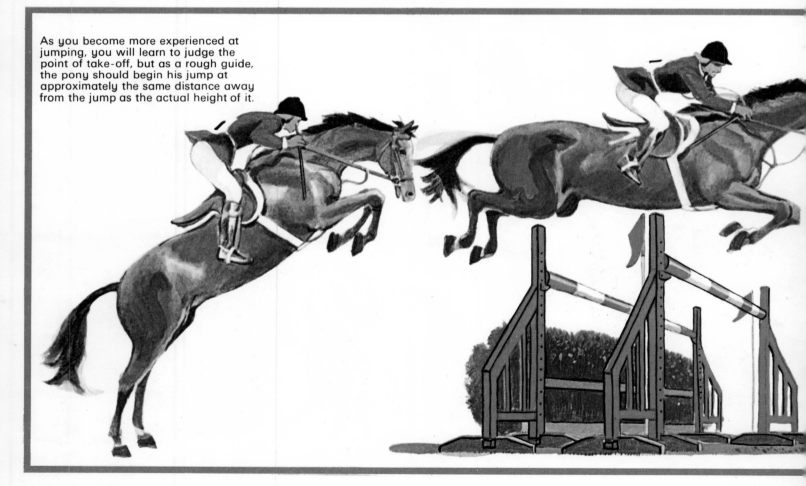

As you become more experienced at jumping, you will learn to judge the point of take-off, but as a rough guide, the pony should begin his jump at approximately the same distance away from the jump as the actual height of it.

Eventing

As your riding improves and you become relaxed and at home on your pony's back, you will probably want to start entering and competing at horse shows. There are all kinds of different classes and competitions — best rider; best turn-out of pony and rider; best working pony and show pony as well as show jumping classes. You will soon find out which you both enjoy most and which you are best at, and now you will realise even more, the importance of keeping your pony and his tack in top condition. As long as he looks clean and neat, happy and well-cared for, you'll find it doesn't matter whether you win or not — you will still be a credit to each other.

Two types of competition that are becoming increasingly popular are Eventing and Combined Training. To compete in these competitions you and your pony don't necessarily need to be an expert in any one field of horsemanship, but you must both be very fit and proficient at a variety of things! In eventing, for example, (which may be held over one or three days), you start out by doing a fairly simple dressage test. That completed and you have to do a 'cross-country' phase. This may involve some road work, and will certainly have a course of 'natural' type fences to jump. These will include hedges, ditches and various rustic jumps similar to obstacles found in the hunting field. Then you have to jump a course of show jumps.

These three events do not directly follow one another. There is time in between for both you and your pony to get your breath back and prepare for the next event. Advanced competitions for very experienced riders, are usually held over three

44

days, the first day for the dressage tests, the second day for cross-country and the third day for the show jumping. Eventing is an exciting and exhilarating event in which to take part.

Combined training is similar to Eventing, except that it misses out the cross-country section, and includes dressage and show jumping events only.

The important point in both types of event, is that it is the *same* pony that does all the phases, so you need a pony that is a good 'all-rounder'. It is no good for example, having a pony that is very good at dressage, if he can't jump well and happily.